# EGGS Everywhere!

# EGGS Everywhere!

Isabel Thomas

Collins

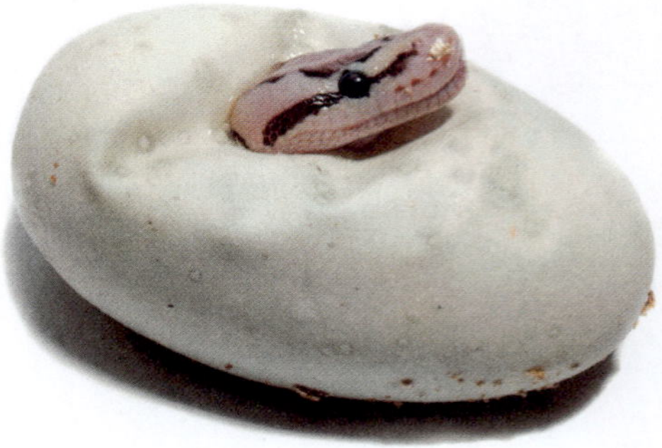

# Contents

Chapter 1 Extraordinary eggs ............... 2

What happens inside an egg? ............... 14

Chapter 2 What came first, the chicken or the egg? ................................. 16

How long do eggs take to hatch? ........... 26

Eggs-treme nests ......................... 28

Chapter 3 Amphibian eggs ................. 30

The mystery of the egg thief ............... 42

Chapter 4 Fish eggs ....................... 44

How many eggs? .......................... 54

Chapter 5 Oceans of eggs .................. 56

Chapter 6 Eggs everywhere ................ 70

Not an egg ............................... 80

Glossary ................................. 84

About the author ......................... 86

Book chat ............................... 88

# Chapter 1
# Extraordinary eggs

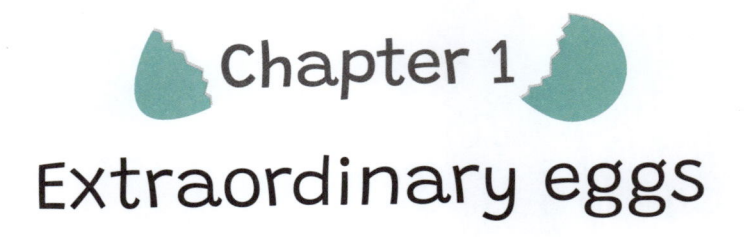

Most animals begin their life inside an egg. Can you spot the eggs in this picture?

That was a trick question ... they are all eggs!

Although animal eggs can be many different shapes, sizes and colours, they all do the same jobs. All eggs provide food and protection for a baby animal as it grows.

The largest eggs are laid by birds. Reptiles, amphibians, fish, insects, and other kinds of animals lay eggs too. There are even two types of mammals that lay eggs.

Eggs are an ordinary part of animal life cycles. But scientists are discovering that eggs are also extraordinary!

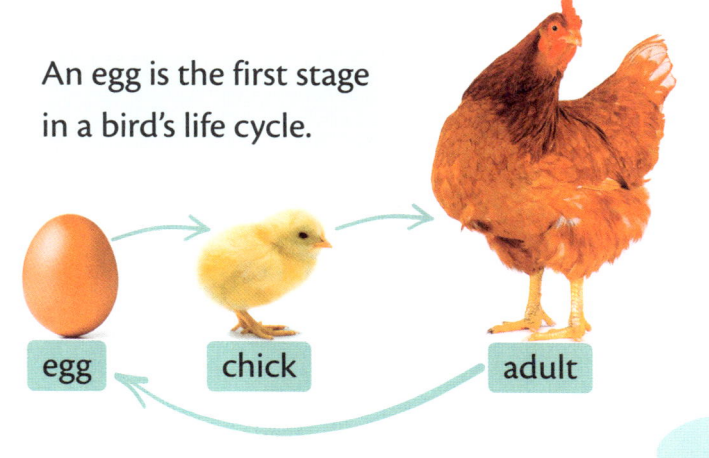

An egg is the first stage in a bird's life cycle.

egg  chick  adult

# Let's "eggs-ray" an egg

Eggs are big business. You can buy them in most food shops. Most people are used to seeing eggs being sold in boxes, like this.

A baby chicken could never grow inside the eggs we buy in shops. These eggs are not **fertilised**. However, they do contain the things a growing chick would need. Next time you see someone cracking open an egg from a shop, see if you can spot these parts.

hard shell to keep water in and germs out

**membranes** let useful things in and keep harmful things out

little ropes hold the yolk in place

yolk provides a chick with food

albumen (egg white) provides a chick with water

tiny holes in the shell let air in and waste out

air pocket provides a chick with air

5

# Eggs-treme sizes

Although all birds' eggs have the same parts, there are many differences. The most obvious difference is size.

Ostriches lay the biggest eggs in the world. Each ostrich egg weighs as much as 24 chicken eggs! Vervain hummingbirds lay the smallest eggs. At just a centimetre tall, each egg is around the size of an adult's fingernail. Ostrich eggs have shells around two millimetres thick. This protects them from predators. Egyptian vultures use rocks to try and break into ostrich eggs for a snack.

Egyptian vulture

vervain hummingbird egg | ostrich egg

Although ostrich eggs are large, they are small compared to the height of an adult ostrich.

Kiwis have much bigger eggs compared to their body size.

x-ray of an egg in a kiwi

# Eggs-quisite colours

*Red and yellow and pink and green, orange and purple and blue ...*

There are more than 10,000 different types of birds, and their eggs are a rainbow of different colours! Scientists have been trying to work out why. There are lots of different ideas.

Birds that nest in colder places tend to lay eggs with darker shells. Darker colours soak up more sunlight, helping to keep the eggs warm.

Birds tend to lay paler eggs in warmer places. The sunlight bounces off paler colours, so the chicks inside the eggs don't get too hot.

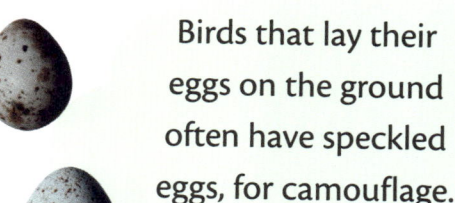

Birds that lay their eggs on the ground often have speckled eggs, for camouflage.

# Egg shapes

What shape is a bird's egg? You might say it's egg-shaped. The scientific name for egg-shaped is "ovoid". However, not all birds' eggs are ovoid! Some are more pointed at the top, like a teardrop. Some are more rounded.

jellybean-shaped hummingbird egg

rounded owl egg

cone-shaped shorebird egg

pointed wading bird egg

## Fact

A sphere is the strongest shape, so why aren't all bird eggs round? Scientists have lots of different ideas to explain this.

Cone-shaped eggs rest bottom-down and stay that way. The top might get covered in the parents' poo, but the bottom stays clean. Chicks can hatch through the clean part.

Cone-shaped eggs fit together better in the nest.

Cone-shaped eggs roll in a circle if they fall out of the nest, so they won't roll off a cliff.

# Eggs-actly right

A chick won't start to grow inside a fertilised bird's egg unless it is warm enough. The best temperature for most bird eggs is 37.5 degrees centigrade which is around the same temperature as our bodies. Although eggs can't make their own warmth, birds can. So, many birds keep their eggs warm by sitting on them!

Most birds have a special patch of skin without feathers. They press this warm skin against the eggs.

Some birds lay just one or two eggs at a time. Others lay more than 20! Birds usually begin **incubating** their eggs once they have all been laid. This means the chicks will hatch at the same time. However, most owls do things differently. They start incubating each egg straight away, so their owlets hatch at different times.

owlets in a nest

# What happens inside an egg?

Once a hen lays a fertilised egg, it takes three weeks for the chick to grow inside.

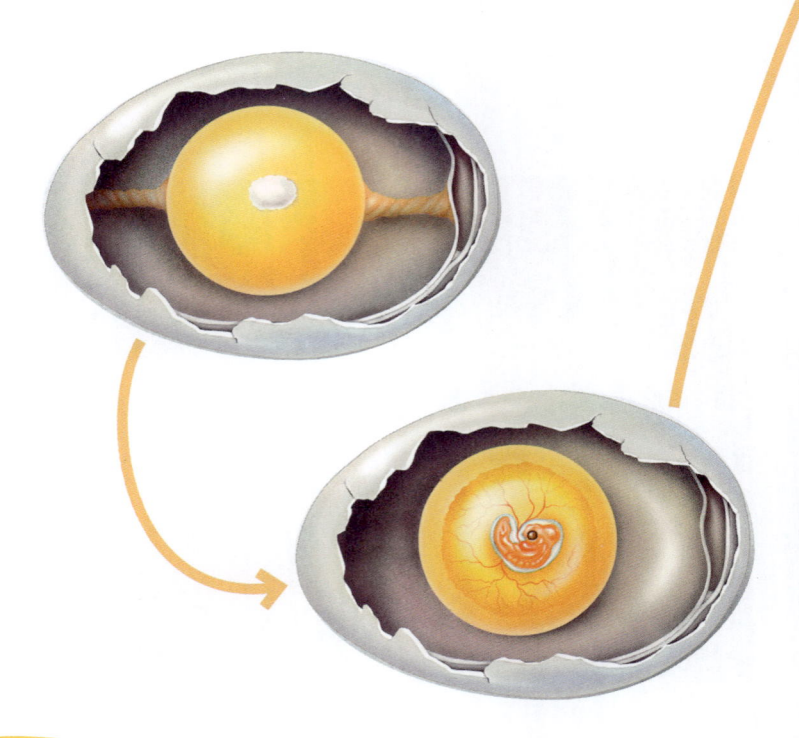

**Fact**

Making the egg in the first place takes just 24 hours. Once the egg is laid, the hen can start making another egg just 30 minutes later!

# Chapter 2

# What came first, the chicken or the egg?

This question sounds tricky, but it's easy to answer once you start looking at fossils.

Dinosaurs are birds' **ancestors**. Fossils show that dinosaurs laid eggs too. This means that eggs came first! Birds have only been on Earth for around 150 million years. But eggs with tough shells and large yolks have been around for at least 300 million years.

### Fact

Dinosaurs also had colourful eggs! Traces of colourful chemicals have been found in nests of fossil dinosaur eggs. They are the same chemicals that give birds' eggs their colours.

Most of today's reptiles lay eggs too. Let's start with the eggs of birds' closest relatives. But creep up carefully …

… it's a crocodile!

As strange as it seems, crocodiles and alligators are the closest living relatives of today's birds.

Like birds, crocodiles lay eggs with hard shells. The eggs need to be kept warm. However, crocodiles don't sit on their eggs to keep them warm. Crocodiles can't heat their own bodies like birds do.

Instead, the mother digs a hole in the ground and covers the eggs with soil. The sun heats the soil and keeps the eggs warm. Some crocodiles build a mound of plants over their eggs. As the plants rot, they heat up. This keeps the eggs warm.

The crocodile guards the nest from predators. When she hears squeaking noises coming from the eggs, she digs them out and helps to open the eggs. She might even carry the hatchlings to water in her mouth!

Hatchling crocodiles have a rough patch of skin on the end of their snouts. This helps them break out of their eggs.

egg

hatchling

adult

crocklet

Other reptiles keep their eggs warm in different ways.

On the Galapagos Islands, some iguanas lay their eggs in the ash inside a volcano crater! This keeps their eggs warm and safe.

Some snakes bask in the sun, then coil their heated bodies around their eggs in a warm hug.

Some turtles and lizards bury their eggs in sand or hide them among rocks that are heated by the sun.

### Fact

For some reptiles, the temperature of the eggs can change how the baby develops. For example, turtle eggs in cooler nests will all hatch as males. Eggs from warmer nests will all hatch as females. American alligator females hatch out of eggs kept at very high or low temperatures. Males hatch out of eggs kept at **mild** temperatures.

Australian brush turkeys use the same trick as crocodiles. Instead of sitting on their eggs, they bury them in mounds of warm, rotting plants.

Unfortunately for the turkeys, reptiles love to eat bird eggs, and this monitor lizard has just found one!

Most reptile eggs don't have hard shells like bird and crocodile eggs. Instead, they are soft, white and rubbery.

These soft-shelled eggs are easier to lay. However, they're also tempting snacks for predators.

**Fact**

You can feel what reptile eggs are like by soaking a chicken egg in a bowl of vinegar for two days. The shell will become so soft, you can bounce the egg like a ball!

## Emergency eggs-it

Not all reptiles stick around to guard their eggs like crocodiles do. So, baby skinks have an emergency exit! If they feel vibrations from a nearby predator, they can hatch early. They burst out of their egg and sprint away!

Green sea turtles return to the sea as soon as they have buried their eggs in the sand. When the baby turtles hatch, they must dash to the sea quickly to avoid being eaten by predators.

# Eggs-tinct reptiles

In 2011, a strange fossil was discovered in Antarctica. No one could work out what it was, although they agreed it looked like a deflated rugby ball. The mysterious object was nicknamed "The Thing".

Recently, scientists realised that The Thing is the fossil egg of a giant prehistoric sea reptile, such as a mosasaur. The egg was probably laid around 68 million years ago.

Mosasaurs may have laid their eggs on land, to stop them being eaten by sea predators. The soft, tough shells would have stopped the eggs drying out.

**Fact**

hen egg

ostrich egg

The Thing

elephant bird egg

The Thing is the second largest egg ever found! The largest belonged to the elephant bird, which is now extinct.

Prehistoric reptiles were the first animals to lay eggs with tough shells. However, they were not the first animals to lay eggs. Their ancestors also laid eggs, of a different kind. You'll meet them in the next chapter.

# How long do eggs take to hatch?

fly 1 day

sardine 1.5 days

spider 14 days

chicken 21 days

python 45 days

emperor penguin 64 days

albatross 80 days

shark 182–274 days (6–9 months)

deep-sea ray 1,095 days (3 years)

giant Pacific octopus 1,460 days (4 years)

27

# Eggs-treme nests

Birds are always hunting for a good nesting spot. Sometimes they end up using human objects.

traffic lights

inside a garden bin

on a statue

inside washing hung on a clothes line

inside a nest made from anti-bird spikes!

inside a traffic cone

If you ever spot a nest in an unusual place, try not to disturb it. You could even put up a sign to warn other people.

# Chapter 3

# Amphibian eggs

The ancestors of reptiles were the very first land animals of all. Amphibians are animals that spend part of their lives in water and part on land.

Prehistoric amphibians probably laid eggs very similar to the ones laid by today's amphibians, such as frogs, toads and newts. You can spot these eggs in ponds in spring.

Amphibians' eggs have no shells and no protective membranes. Although most adult amphibians live on land, they must lay their eggs in a wet place or the eggs will dry out.

Although a frog's eggs don't have a shell, they do have a coating of jelly to protect them. The jelly starts to swell up after the eggs have been laid. The black dot at the centre is the developing baby frog.

A cluster of frogs' eggs is known as frogspawn.

A newly hatched frog is called a tadpole. It looks nothing like an adult frog. As the tadpole develops, its body changes completely. It changes from an underwater creature to a creature that can live on land.

Frogs lay eggs.

after one hour

Jelly around the eggs swells to make frogspawn.

after two to three weeks

Tadpoles hatch. They have long tails and **gills** (like a fish) to breathe underwater. At first, they eat plants.

after eight weeks

Tadpoles grow back legs, and begin to hunt prey.

Tadpole's gills disappear and they begin to breathe air. They grow front legs.

Young frog's tail disappears.

after two to three years

Adult frog ready to lay eggs of its own.

## So many eggs

Frogs can lay up to 5,000 eggs at a time! They lay so many because watery places like ponds are full of predators, such as fish. Even tadpoles like to eat frogspawn – and each other!

Not many of a frog's eggs will survive to be tadpoles. Even fewer will become adult frogs.

Only around one in every 50 of a frog's eggs will survive to adulthood. This is why woodlands, parks and gardens aren't hopping with thousands of frogs!

Some frogs and toads lay fewer eggs and stick around to protect them. They help keep their eggs safe in different ways.

a great diving beetle larva attacks a tadpole

Which of these amphibians do you think deserves the star parent award?

A father midwife toad carries eggs around on his legs. He takes them to the water when it's time to hatch.

A mother Surinam toad's skin grows around her eggs on her back. After 80 days, she sheds her old skin and the young toads are released.

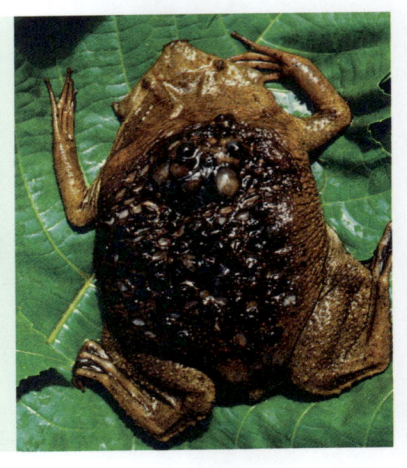

Male strawberry poison dart frogs try to eat each other's eggs. The males wrestle with each other to protect their own eggs.

Male Darwin's frogs guard their eggs inside their throats. When the froglets are ready, they hop out of their father's mouth.

Poison arrow frogs lay their eggs on leaves or branches, away from water predators. One parent guards the eggs and keeps them wet by weeing on them.

Newts and salamanders are amphibians with tails. They begin their lives as tadpoles, just like frogs. Newts lay their eggs on underwater plants. They often fold leaves around their eggs, to hide them.

Axolotls are unusual salamanders that don't change from tadpoles to adults. They keep their frilly gills and live underwater for their whole lives.

Axolotls lay eggs in deep water, hidden from fish among underwater plants. The **larvae** hatch before they are ready to find their own food. The larvae keep the yolk of their egg with them, and eat this during their first week. It's as if they are eggs on the move!

Most amphibians must find water to lay their eggs. But some have found clever ways to keep their eggs wet on land.

In rainforests, frogs seek out tiny pools of water hidden inside plants.

Foam-nest tree frogs lay their eggs on trees that grow over water. Using their feet, the frogs churn **mucus** into a frothy foam to cover the eggs. The foam keeps the eggs moist until the tadpoles hatch and drop into the water below.

Tungara frogs build foamy mucus nests that float on the water – like little rafts.

Bubble-nest frogs lay their eggs inside hollow stalks of bamboo. The father guards the eggs until they hatch.

Giant burrowing frogs lay their eggs in burrows dug by other creatures. The tadpoles have to wait for a flood to escape their underground holes!

Kumbara night frogs do handstands to lay their eggs on twigs. Then they smear the eggs with mud using their back legs.

# The mystery of the egg thief

# Egg thief!

In 1923, scientists made an amazing discovery: a nest of 13 fossil eggs. These were the first dinosaur eggs ever discovered. They had been buried in a sandstorm more than 65 million years ago.

Next to the sandy nest, they found the bones of a small meat-eating dinosaur. They thought it had been robbing the nest when the sandstorm struck, and called the dinosaur Oviraptor, meaning "egg thief".

Today, scientists think that Oviraptor was not to blame. The eggs were actually her own eggs. She probably died protecting her nest.

# Chapter 4

# Fish eggs

Amphibians weren't the first animals to lay eggs. Their ancestors were fish, which have been laying eggs for almost 500 million years.

Fish can't escape the water to lay their eggs on land, like many amphibians do. How do fish make sure their eggs survive in the sea?

For most ocean fish, the secret is to lay lots and lots and LOTS of tiny eggs. A swordfish can release millions of eggs in one go!

fish releasing clouds of eggs

Eggs laid in the open ocean don't stay in one place. They soon drift away. The parent fish will never meet their young and won't look after them.

When they hatch, swordfish **fry** are just four millimetres long, with tiny snouts. At first, they can only eat **plankton**.

Out of millions of eggs, only a few will survive to become adult fish. But this is enough to keep the swordfish family tree going.

Some ocean fish try to give their young a head start by laying their eggs in a safer place than the middle of the sea. So, they head back to the shallow rivers where they began their lives.

To get back, Pacific salmon swim hundreds of kilometres up rivers, leap up waterfalls and dodge grizzly bears.

alevin (newly-spawned salmon)

egg

yolk sac

adult (**spawning**)

When a mother fish finally reaches the river where she hatched, she hollows out a nest in the riverbed with her tail. Once the eggs have been laid and fertilised, she covers them with gravel.

About one in every hundred salmon eggs survive to become adult fish.

fry

smolt (young salmon)

adult (ocean)

Not all fish leave their eggs. Three-spined sticklebacks build a nest of weeds, stuck together with mucus. The eggs are laid inside the nest. The father fish guards guards them until they hatch.

three-spined stickleback and nest

Cichlids go a step further and keep their eggs safe in their mouths. The yellow-headed jawfish does the same, spitting its eggs out when it eats, then sucking them back in again.

Male seahorses have
a special pouch above
their tails, which can fit
up to a thousand eggs.
The skin of
the seahorse's belly
changes so food and
**oxygen** can reach
the developing eggs.

male seahorse with eggs

Most sharks also keep their eggs safe inside
their own bodies. The young sharks hatch out
while they are still in their mother's body, and
swim out when they are big enough to survive on
their own.

A few types of sharks do lay eggs, but they
don't look like any other kind of egg you've
ever seen …

Next time you visit a beach, look out for a "mermaid's purse" washed up on the shore.

These are the empty egg cases of sharks and rays. Each one is about the size of your palm. It once contained a developing baby shark, and a yolk full of food.

The size and shape of an egg case can help you to work out who it belonged to. Some shark egg cases have long curly tendrils for attaching the egg to seaweed or rocks. Ray egg cases often have "horns" at the corners.

Strangest of all are the spiral-shaped eggs of the Port Jackson shark. The mother shark picks up her eggs in her mouth and screws them into gaps between rocks. This protects the eggs and makes sure they don't get washed away.

# Empty egg cases

bullhead shark

catshark

nursehound

ray

draughtsboard shark

Port Jackson shark

It might seem risky to leave your eggs in the ocean. Sharks are predators, but their eggs are at risk of being eaten too. Not by other sharks, but by sea snails! Snails bore holes through the leathery egg case and suck out the contents.

However, scientists are discovering that being eaten by predators isn't always the end for an egg.

## Eggs-periment

In an experiment, eight mallard ducks were given food containing around 500 fish eggs – the kind of eggs that would normally be on the plants that ducks like to eat.

When the scientists checked the ducks' poo, they found 18 eggs that hadn't been digested. Three of these hatched into baby fish.

mallard ducks eating

So, now we know that some fish eggs can be eaten and pooped out by a duck and still hatch into healthy fish.

This could help to explain a mystery – how fish came to live in lakes and ponds that are many kilometres from other water. Ducks might accidentally eat eggs in one place, then fly to another lake and poop them out.

# How many eggs?

Some animals lay huge numbers of eggs – but nothing beats the ocean sunfish!

ocean sunfish: 300 million eggs

bluefin tuna: 10 million eggs

blue crab: 8 million eggs

ant: 4 million eggs

sea urchin: 2 million eggs

cone snail: 1.5 million eggs

sea nettle: 40 thousand eggs

cane toad: 35 thousand eggs

# Chapter 5
# Oceans of eggs

Fish eggs aren't the only eggs floating around in the ocean. Millions of other sea creatures lay eggs too. Some of these can be spotted on the shore.

Paddleworm eggs look like jelly blobs.

Sea hare eggs look like spaghetti.

dog whelk eggs

cushion sea star eggs

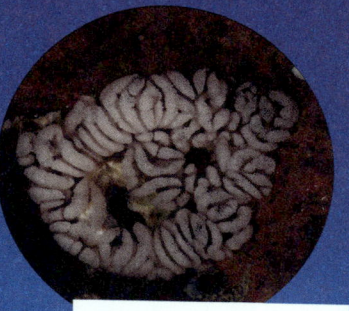

grey sea slug eggs

Periwinkles lay their eggs on seaweed.

Sea wash balls are the empty egg cases of the common whelk. Sailors once collected them to use as sponges.

Cuttlefish eggs look like little bunches of black grapes.

57

Many eggs get washed up onto beaches by accident, but some are left there on purpose.

Every spring, hundreds of thousands of Atlantic horseshoe crabs crawl onto beaches at night to lay their eggs. Each horseshoe crab lays about 20,000 eggs per night. Most of these get eaten by sea birds, turtles and fish.

crowds of horseshoe crabs on a beach

# Eggs and legs

Horseshoe crabs aren't really crabs. They are more closely related to spiders.

Even more confusingly, sea spiders aren't really spiders! They are strange sea creatures with huge legs and tiny bodies. Female sea spiders lay eggs from their legs! Some male sea spiders carry the fertilised eggs on their legs, to protect them.

sea spider carrying eggs on legs

## Caring crabs

You won't find the eggs of crabs and lobsters scattered on a beach. Most **crustaceans** carry their eggs beneath their bodies in special pouches.

The cluster of eggs is often bright orange, yellow, purple or red. It stays attached until the eggs hatch.

crab with eggs held under it

The larvae that hatch from a crab's eggs don't look anything like their parents. As they grow and develop, their appearance changes. Each stage has a different name.

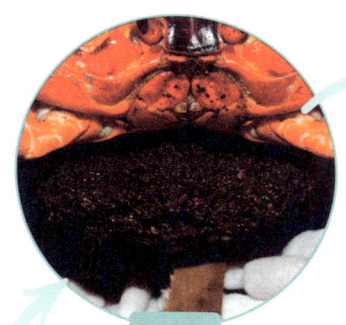

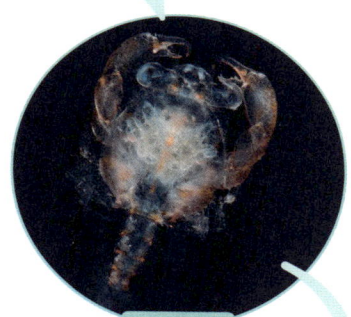

- eggs
- larvae
- megalops
- juvenile
- adult crab

# Marine molluscs

Sea snail shells are even tougher than a crustacean's shell. However, their eggs are not so lucky. Most sea snails lay lots of soft eggs that float around in the open ocean.

Conches lay ribbons of eggs up to 23 metres long. Each ribbon contains almost half a million eggs.

a whelk laying eggs

Being stuck together provides some protection, but it brings risks too. The first common whelks to hatch gobble their unhatched brothers and sisters as their first meal!

Sea slugs are close relatives of sea snails. Although they don't have shells, sea slugs are protected by being poisonous. Their bright colours warn predators to stay away.

Sea slugs lay eggs in ribbons or strings. They look like beautiful flowers on the ocean floor. However, you wouldn't want to pick them. Sea slug eggs can be as **toxic** as their parents, thanks to a layer of venomous snot!

a nudibranch sea slug egg ribbon

Octopuses are giant marine molluscs. A giant Pacific octopus lays eggs only once in her lifetime, then guards them until they hatch – which can take up to four years! During that time, the mother octopus never moves – not even to find food.

Other types of octopus speed incubation up, by finding a warm place to lay their eggs. The warmest places in the ocean are around underwater volcanoes. Scientists found nearly 6,000 pearl octopuses huddled around one underwater volcano near California, USA. The warm water halved the time it took their eggs to hatch.

giant Pacific octopus guarding her eggs

65

Like octopuses, squid are also marine molluscs with soft bodies, large eyes and eight arms. However, squid don't guard their eggs like octopuses do. Some types of squid glue their finger-shaped eggs to rocks or seaweed.

Other squid lay eggs coated in jelly, which soaks up water and swells up. Divers have come across balls of squid eggs as large as a car! The jelly coating protects the developing eggs from predators.

Sometimes clusters of squid eggs are knocked off rocks and wash up on beaches.

squid eggs

# Rule breakers

Jellyfish have been around far longer than dinosaurs, fish, or molluscs. They were some of the very first animals on Earth. So jellyfish eggs were probably some of the first eggs ever laid.

Eggs are laid by adult jellyfish, known as medusa. However, jellyfish have a strange life cycle compared to other animals.

A young jellyfish can detach a piece of itself to make a new jellyfish. This unusual life cycle means that a jellyfish could be **immortal**, if it can avoid predators for long enough.

adult

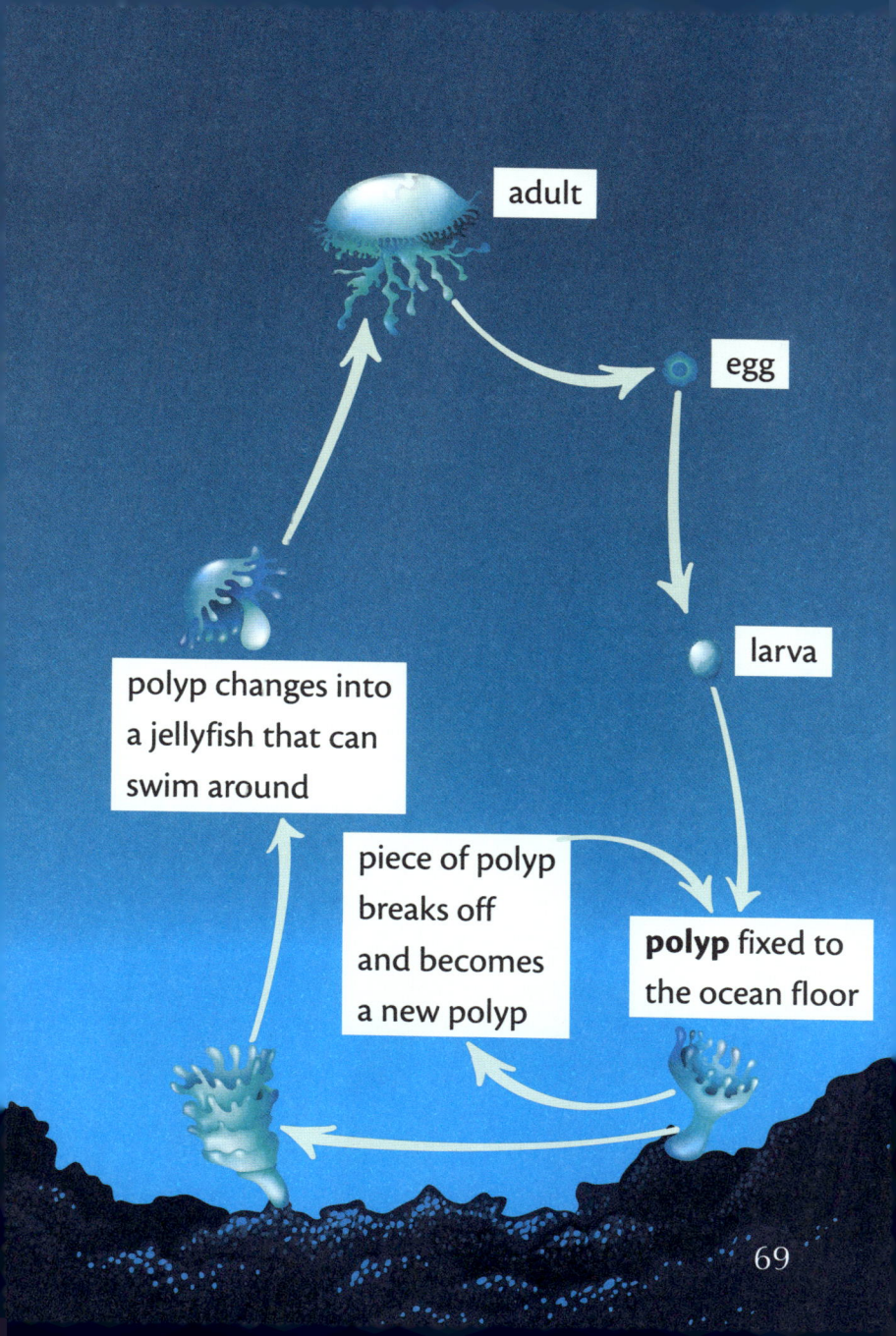

egg

larva

**polyp** fixed to the ocean floor

piece of polyp breaks off and becomes a new polyp

polyp changes into a jellyfish that can swim around

69

# Chapter 6

# Eggs everywhere

Most animals in the world are insects, and almost all insects lay eggs. Eggs laid on land are more likely to stay in one place, compared with eggs laid at sea. So some insects lay their eggs on a source of food, so their young can eat the food when they hatch.

Most butterflies lay their eggs on edible plants. Red admirals choose stinging nettles, which are less likely to be eaten by big **herbivores**, such as cows and horses.

egg → caterpillar → pupa → adult

There are thousands of different types of wasps, and most don't build nests. Instead, they lay their eggs on another small animal. For example, potter wasps trap caterpillars inside tiny "pots" made from mud. Then the potter wasps lay their eggs on top of the caterpillar. When the wasp eggs hatch, the young wasps eat the caterpillar.

Dung beetles lay their eggs in the freshest, juiciest dung they can find. It will be a feast for the young beetles when they hatch!

Many insects also find different ways to protect their eggs from predators.

# Eggs-actly the same

Stick insects lay eggs that look exactly like plant seeds. They even have a knobbly part, like real seeds. Ants are tricked into carrying these eggs into their nests, thinking they are just getting a tasty snack. The ants eat the knobbly part, which is full of fat, but leave the rest uneaten. The egg remains inside the ants' nest, safe from predators, until it hatches.

Green lacewings lay their eggs on leaves, dangling from the ends of silk threads like baubles. This stops hungry ants and other insects from spotting them.

green lacewing eggs under a leaf

Black fire beetles are one of the few animals that dash *towards* a forest fire! They lay their eggs in freshly burnt trees. When the larvae hatch, they can feed on burnt wood. No one else is eating the burnt wood, and there are no predators around!

black fire beetle

## Mysterious molluscs

Molluscs live on land as well as in the sea. They include snails and slugs. Like sea slugs, some land snails lay toxic eggs.

## Poison apple

Apple snails spend most of their lives in fresh water but crawl out of the water to lay eggs on plants or rocks.

Apple snail eggs are much easier to spot than the snails themselves. They are bright pink! This is a warning that they are toxic to almost every animal, including humans. Only fire ants can eat apple snail eggs (though no one knows how).

Tropical blinking snails have even odder eggs that make their own light and glow in the dark! The adult snails can give off flashes of green light too. No one yet knows why they glow.

apple snail eggs

There are many different types of mammals, including humans. Most mammals don't lay eggs. Baby mammals grow inside their mother's body. However, two types of mammals break this rule.

## Eggs-tra cute

Echidnas lay eggs the size of grapes, with soft, leathery shells. The eggs roll into a special pouch on the mother's belly. After ten days, a tiny baby echidna (called a puggle) hatches. It is about the size of a jellybean. The puggle lives in the mother's pouch, drinking her milk, until it's big enough to be left in the burrow.

echidna

puggle

Platypuses lay their eggs straight into their burrows. To keep the eggs safe and warm, the mother curls around the eggs.

Like birds and reptiles, puggles have an egg tooth to help them break out of their eggs.

puggle

These unusual egg-laying mammals only live in Australia, New Guinea, Tasmania and Indonesia.

# Eggs-pert knowledge

Although scientists have discovered a lot, they would say they have only just started to crack the mysteries of animal eggs.

In the past, scientists used to collect eggs they found, to take a thorough look. These old eggs are still on display in museums.

Charles Darwin collected 16 birds' eggs on his famous *Beagle* voyage.

Today, scientists know that we should never take or disturb eggs that we find in the wild. This harms animals. In many parts of the world, it's against the law to take birds' eggs from the wild.

We can protect animals AND find out more about eggs by watching them hatch in the places where they are laid. Technology such as nest cameras can help with this. Look closely at what's happening in your garden, your local park, or the school playground, and you could make some eggs-traordinary discoveries too!

# Not an egg

All these things look like eggs – but aren't. Can you guess what they are? Find the answers on page 82.

A

B

C

80

D

E

F

81

# Answers

A

The fried egg jellyfish just happens to look like a favourite breakfast food.

B

Passion flower leaves have spots that look like butterfly eggs. This stops butterflies from laying real eggs on the leaves, which stops caterpillars hatching out and eating the leaves.

C

Male darter fish have fake eggs on their fins. These help them to attract female fish.

D

These all look like termite eggs, but the orange ones are really balls of **fungi**. The termites are fooled into looking after the fungus, as well as their eggs.

E

Geodes are rocks shaped like eggs. They are even nicknamed "thunder eggs". They are hollow at the centre, and often contain layers of beautiful crystals.

F

The "Easter egg" eggplant (aubergine) has small ovoid fruits that look just like little eggs.

# Glossary

**ancestors**  relations that lived in the past

**crustaceans**  creatures such as crabs and lobsters, often found in water, that have a hard shell covering their bodies

**fertilised**  when parts of two parent animals combine, creating an egg that can grow into a new animal

**fry**  very young fish

**fungi**  living things, such as mushrooms, that get their food from decaying plants and other living things

**gills**  the organs that fish and other creatures use to breathe

**herbivores**  animals that eat plants

**immortal**  living forever

**incubating**  keeping eggs warm until they hatch

**larvae** the early forms of insects or other animals that look quite different from their adult form; for example, caterpillars are the larvae of butterflies

**membranes** thin, bendy layers or barriers that separate different parts of a living thing

**mild** moderate, not extreme

**mucus** slimy substance that moistens and protects

**oxygen** a gas that most living things need to survive

**plankton** tiny living creatures that float or drift in water

**polyp** an early stage of a jellyfish's life cycle

**spawning** releasing lots of eggs at once

**toxic** poisonous

# About the author

**How did you become a science writer?**

At school, my favourite subjects were Science and Maths. I studied Science at university, learning all about animal behaviour, evolution and physiology (how animals' bodies work). I also wrote for a student newspaper. After university, I found a job that combined the things I loved best — science and writing!

**Isabel Thomas**

**What is it like for you to write?**

It feels like doing a jigsaw puzzle when you don't know what the final picture will look like. I concentrate so much that I forget about everything else. I'm always moving words and sentences around, until everything fits perfectly.

**What's your favourite thing about writing?**

When I'm dreaming up new ideas for a book, or when I've finished writing a book. The part in the middle can feel tricky, but it's worth it when you finish a project.

**What's the most amazing egg you've ever seen?**

I have two rescue tortoises, and I was amazed when one laid an egg. I thought it might be a bird's egg that had rolled onto the floor, but it was perfectly spherical. As we only have female tortoises, the egg wasn't fertilised so no baby tortoise was growing inside.

**Why did you decide to write this book?**

I was amazed when my tortoise laid a round egg, I'd never seen a reptile's egg before. So, I began wondering what kind of eggs other animals laid and how they differ from birds' eggs, which I'm more used to seeing. I love writing about something that is new to me, because the research feels like going on an adventure into the unknown.

**What do you hope readers will learn from the book?**

I hope readers will learn that eggs are just as diverse as the animals that lay them. Studying eggs is an important part of understanding nature better. Another important message is that we shouldn't disturb eggs we spot in the wild. Animals go to such an effort to protect their eggs and we can help them survive by leaving them alone.

**What's the most amazing fact you discovered while writing this book?**

Many animals hide or camouflage their eggs, but not apple snails. They are bright pink and laid in clusters of hundreds. They are also poisonous, even to humans. When you see something brightly coloured in nature, it's often a warning to leave it alone!

# Book chat

When you looked at the cover of the book, what did you think it would be about? Did you change your mind as you read it?

Does this book remind you of any other books you've read? How?

Have you ever seen any of the eggs mentioned in this book?

What's the most interesting thing you learnt from reading this book?

What was your favourite egg in the book?

Did anything really surprise you in the book?

If you could ask the author one question, what would you ask?

Would you recommend this book? Why or why not?

What egg or animal from this book would you most like to see and why?

If someone asked you to describe what this book was about, what would you say?

If you could give the author one piece of advice to improve the book, what would it be?

What part of the book did you like best and why?

If you could learn more about one animal from this book, which one would you choose and why?

**Book challenge:**
Draw and label your own amazing egg and the animal that would hatch from it.

**Collins BIG CAT**

Published by Collins An imprint of HarperCollins*Publishers*

The News Building
1 London Bridge Street
London
SE1 9GF
UK

Macken House
39/40 Mayor Street Upper
Dublin 1
D01 C9W8
Ireland

© HarperCollins*Publishers* Limited 2024

10 9 8 7 6 5 4 3 2 1

ISBN 978-0-00-868116-6

All rights reserved. No part of this publication may be reproduced, stored in a retrieval system, or transmitted in any form by any means, electronic, mechanical, photocopying, recording or otherwise, without the prior written permission of the Publisher or a licence permitting restricted copying in the United Kingdom issued by the Copyright Licensing Agency Ltd, 5th Floor, Shackleton House, 4 Battle Bridge Lane, London SE1 2HX.

British Library Cataloguing-in-Publication Data
A catalogue record for this publication is available from the British Library.

Download the teaching notes and word cards to accompany this book at: http://littlewandle.org.uk/signupfluency/

**Get the latest Collins Big Cat news at**
collins.co.uk/collinsbigcat

Author: Isabel Thomas
Illustrator: Caitlin O'Dwyer (Astound Illustration Agency)
Publisher: Laura White
Product manager: Caroline Green
Series editor: Charlotte Raby
Development editor: Catherine Baker
Commissioning editor: Suzannah Ditchburn
Project manager: Emily Hooton
Copyeditor: Sally Byford
Picture researcher: Sophie Hartley
Proofreader: Catherine Dakin
Cover designer: Sarah Finan
Typesetter: 2Hoots Publishing Services Ltd
Production controller: Katharine Willard

Printed in the UK.

**MIX**
Paper | Supporting responsible forestry
FSC™ C007454
www.fsc.org

This book is produced from independently certified FSC™ paper to ensure responsible forest management.

For more information visit: www.harpercollins.co.uk/green

Made with responsibly sourced paper and vegetable ink

Scan to see how we are reducing our environmental impact.

Acknowledgements
The publishers gratefully acknowledge the permission granted to reproduce the copyright material in this book. Every effort has been made to trace copyright holders and to obtain their permission for the use of copyright material. The publishers will gladly receive any information enabling them to rectify any error or omission at the first opportunity.

p2bl Dorling Kindersley Ltd/Alamy, p2br Arterra Picture Library/Alamy, p6 ZUMA Press, Inc./Alamy, p7c DPA Picture Alliance/Alamy, p7b Natalia Lashmanova/Alamy, p10 Paul R. Sterry/Alamy, p12 Nature Picture Library/Alamy, p13 Minden Pictures/Alamy, pp14–15 Laurie O'Keefe/Science Photo Library, p19t Sergey Gorshkov/Nature Picture Library, p20t, Tui De Roy/Minden Pictures/Nature Picture Library, p20c BIOSPHOTO/Alamy, p20b James L. Peacock/Alamy, p21t WILDLIFE GmbH/Alamy, p21b Gerry Pearce/Alamy, p23b Avalon.red/Alamy, p24 Mark Garlick/Science Photo Library, p25bc Natural History Museum, London/Science Photo Library, p25b Christian Becker/MNHM Chile, p27bcl Brian Skerry/Minden/Nature Picture Library, p36b BIOSPHOTO/Alamy, p37t Marek Stefunko/Alamy, p37c Minden Pictures/Alamy, p37b Helmut Göthel Symbiosis/Alamy, p38 Andy Newman/Alamy, p39 Mark Boulton/Alamy, p40t RooM the Agency/Alamy, p40c&b Minden Pictures/Alamy, p41t Chien Lee/Minden/Nature Picture Library, pp42 & 43t Julius T Csotonyi/Science Photo Library, p43b Photostock-Israel/Science Photo Library, p44 Nature Picture Library/Alamy, p45 Blue Planet Archive/Alamy, p46tl&tr Minden Pictures/Alamy, p46b Zoonar GmbH/Alamy, p47t Felix Choo/Alamy, p47c NatPar Collection/Alamy, p47b Fernando Lessa/Alamy, p48 Blickwinkel/Alamy, p49 Tony Wu/Nature Picture Library, p51tl Andy Murch/Nature Picture Library, p51tr Arterra Picture Library/Alamy, p51cl Nature Picture Library/Alamy, p51cr Nature Picture Partners/Alamy, p51bl Jane Rix/Alamy, p51br Oreolife/Alamy, p53 Simon R B Brown/Alamy, p56tl Pix/Alamy, p56tr WaterFrame/Alamy, p57tl Tony Wu/Nature Picture Library, p57tr Robin Chittenden/Alamy, p57c imageBROKER.com GmbH & Co. KG/Alamy, p57bl Nature Picture Library/Alamy, p57br Nathaniel Noir/Alamy, p58 Mark Burnett/Alamy, p59, Christophe Courteau/Nature Picture Library, p61cl imageBROKER.com GmbH & Co. KG/Alamy, p61tl Reinhard Dirscherl/Alamy, p61bl WaterFrame/Alamy, p61tr Dante Fenolio/Science Photo Library, p61br Gerd Guenther/Science Photo Library, p62 Blickwinkel/Alamy, p65 Minden Pictures/Alamy, p68 Alexander Semenov/Science Photo Library, p70l Dorling Kindersley Ltd/Alamy, p70cr Malcolm Schuyl/Alamy, p71t Mauritius Images GmbH/Alamy, pp76t & 77r Minden Pictures/Alamy, p79 Tierfotoagentur/Alamy, p80tr Geoff Kidd/Science Photo Library/Alamy, p80b Archive PL/Alamy, p81t Doug Wechsler/Nature Picture Library, p82c Geoff Kidd/Science Photo Library/Alamy, p82b Archive PL/Alamy, p83t Doug Wechsler/Nature Picture Library. All other photos Shutterstock.